P9-CUK-577

The Usborne Book of

Monster
Jokes

CONTENTS

Designed and
illustrated by
Leonard Le Rolland

Edited by
Laura Howell

4

Deadly dinners

Monster 1: Am I late for dinner?
Monster 2: Yes, everyone's been eaten.

Little monster: I don't like Grandpa.
Mother monster: Well, just leave him on the side of your plate.

Girl monster: Dad, I want to get married.
Dad monster: Have you found an edible bachelor?

Little monster: I've finished eating, may I leave the table?
Mother monster: Of course, I'll save it for your supper.

Mary Monster: I don't know what to make of my husband.
Myra Monster: How about a pie?

Did you hear about the monster restaurant?
Dinner costs an arm and a leg.

What did the mother monster say
to her son at the dinner table?
"Don't speak with someone in your mouth!"

Little monster: Should I eat chicken with my fingers?
Mother monster: No, you should eat the
fingers separately.

...d taste

Did you hear about the monster who ate
nothing but little pieces of metal?
It was his staple diet.

Monster 1: I don't think much of your wife.
Monster 2: Hmm, maybe she's overcooked.

Frankie Monster: My dad's so tough, he
wrestled an alligator then bit off its head.
Benjy Monster: Well, my dad's so tough,
we boiled him for ten hours and he
still gave us indigestion.

Did you hear about the monster
who dreamed he was chewing a bone?
When he woke up he only had one leg.

Little monster: Mother, I've
brought a friend home for dinner.
Mother monster: How thoughtful.
Will she fit in the oven?

Mr. Monster: Hurry up and cook my dinner!
Mrs. Monster: Oh, stop complaining –
I've only got four pairs of hands.

Monster 1: Who was that lady I
saw you with yesterday?
Monster 2: That was no lady,
that was my lunch.

Pleased to eat you

Monster 1: I've just bought a new refrigerator.
Monster 2: Does it hold a lot?
Monster 1: Well, the two delivery men fitted inside.

What does a monster call a person in a hammock?

Breakfast in bed.

Why don't monsters eat clowns?

They taste funny.

What does a monster call people with skateboards?

Meals on wheels.

Did you hear about the monster who was thrown off a cruise ship?
At dinner, he asked for the passenger list instead of the menu.

Why didn't the monster eat the crazy person?
He was allergic to nuts.

Monster 1: We had burglars last night.
Monster 2: Were they tasty?

What do you get if you cross a monster with a dog?
A creature that bites people, then buries the bones.

What does a monster call a
train full of passengers?
A chew-chew train.

Did you hear about the monsters
that ate some comedians?
It was a feast of fun.

Did you hear about the monster
who wanted fast food?
He ordered a pizza with everyone on it.

How can you help a starving monster?
Give him a hand.

What do monsters like to
do at weddings?
Toast the bride
and groom.

What kind of beans do monsters like to eat?

Human beans.

What does a monster call a team of athletes?

A running buffet.

Have you ever seen a man-eating monster?

No, but I've seen a woman eating fudge.

Don't feed the monsters!

What did the monster say when he had only a small, spiky plant for dinner?
"Thistle have to do."

Why did the monster eat a candle?
For a little light refreshment.

Where do monsters go for dinner?
To a beastro.

I'VE GOT A STOMACHACHE...

How do you fit a monster in a refrigerator?
Take out the milk.

How do you know if someone's put a
monster in your refrigerator?
The door won't close and the milk's turned sour.

When are monsters most likely to eat raw meat?
On Chews-day.

When are monsters most likely to eat cooked meat?
On Fried-day.

...MAYBE IT WAS SOMEONE YOU ATE!

Beware of the monsters

What should you do if a monster breaks down your front door?
Escape through the back door.

What's even louder than an angry monster?
Ten angry monsters.

What's even louder than ten angry monsters?
Ten angry monsters with trumpets.

How fast do you have to run when a monster's chasing you?
Faster than the monster.

What's the difference between a furious monster and a teacher?
You can reason with a monster.

What time is it when you see a monster?
Time to run.

What sport are monsters best at?

Squash.

Monster allsorts

Why do monsters paint their claws red?
So they can hide in cherry trees.

Why are monsters big and purple?
Because if they were small and green, you'd
mistake them for gooseberries.

Monster: Doctor, I keep thinking I'm a bridge.
Doctor: What on earth's come over you?
Monster: Ten cars, three trucks and a bus.

Billy: I lost my pet monster.
Bobby: Why don't you put an ad in the newspaper?
Billy: Don't be silly, he can't read.

What happened when the
monster took a taxi home?
He had to give it back.

Did you hear about the hairy
monster who met a werewolf?
They became beast friends.

What do you call a big, green monster
who sits on his own in the corner?
The Incredible Sulk.

How many monsters does it
take to change a lightbulb?
Two. One to change the bulb,
and another to eat the old one.

How many monsters can you fit in a car?
I don't know, but you can fit about
ten cars in a monster.

How do you tell the difference between
a monster and a football?
Try picking them up.

Where do monsters live?
In monstrocities.

Why did the chicken cross the road?
It was stuck to the sole of a monster's foot.

Monster 1: I was at the zoo last week.
Monster 2: Which cage were you in?

What's big and ugly and
goes up and down?
A monster on a trampoline.

A sight for sore eyes

Mickey Monster: That cute girl over there just rolled her eyes at me.
Malcolm Monster: You'd better roll them back, she might need them.

Dirk: A monster just bit my arm.
Kirk: Did you put anything on it?
Dirk: No, he seemed to like it as it was.

Doctor: What seems to be the problem?
Monster: I've seen five doctors and none of them could make me feel better, so I ate them.
Doctor: How unfortunate... um, I'm a plumber.

What's the difference between a monster
and crazy Aunt Mabel?
One's a huge, ugly, savage creature and
the other's a monster.

What happened when the
monster swallowed Big Ben?
He found it time-consuming.

Knock knock.

Who's there?

Dallas.

Dallas who?

Dallas time I saw such a hideous
face, it belonged to a monster.

What do you call the squishy stuff
between a monster's toes?
Slow runners.

What do you get if you cross a
monster and a parrot?
Something that bites off your head,
then says, "Who's a pretty boy?"

Absolutely hideous

Did you hear about the monster who was so huge, he fell in the Grand Canyon and got stuck?

Did you hear about the monster who was so ugly, he got in a bathtub and the water jumped out?

Did you hear about the monster who was so dirty, she lost weight every time she showered?

Did you hear about the monster who was so slimy, even her spots slid off?

Did you hear about the monster who was so smelly, he made onions cry?

How do monsters
burst their pimples?
With a hammer.

Who won the monster
beauty contest?
No one.

What's purple and
runs very slowly?
A monster's nose.

27

Monster bodies

What goes stomp, clonk?
A monster with a wooden leg.

What's as sharp as a monster's tooth?
His other teeth.

What do you call a monster with no legs?
Anything you like. He can't chase you.

What did the monster say when the
dentist finished filling her teeth?
"Fangs a lot!"

What looks like
half a monster?
The other half.

Did you hear about the monster
who had ten arms and no legs?
He was all fingers and thumbs.

28

Why is a monster's
nose in the middle
of its face?
Because it's
the scenter.

What can never
be made right?
A monster's left eye.

What's red and squishy
and weighs ten tons?
An inside-out monster.

Tops and tails

What does a monster do if it loses its tail?
Goes to the retail store.

Why did the poor monster chase its tail?
To make ends meet.

Why should you never try to
catch a monster by his tail?
It's the end of the monster and
it'll be the end of you too.

Why can you never misbehave in
a monster teacher's class?
Because she has eyes in the back of her heads.

What happened to the monster who had a
strawberry growing out of his head?
The doctor gave him some cream for it.

What does a monster do when she loses her head?
Calls a head hunter.

What do you call a monster with a wooden head?
Edward.

What's got three heads and two tails?
A monster tossing a coin.

What do you call...

... an insect that lives in
a graveyard?
A zom-bee.

... a one-eyed monster
with a pastry crust?
Pieclops.

... a giant monster that
likes to poke people?
Prodzilla.

... a monster ape with a bell on his head?
Ding Dong.

... a monster dog that likes sports?
The Hound of the Basketballs.

What do you get...

... **if you cross a monster with a kangaroo?**
I don't know, but don't let it jump on your toes.

... **if you cross a monster with a computer?**
A big mac.

... **if you cross a ten-ton monster with a cookie?**
A pile of crumbs.

... **if you cross a monster with a camera?**
A snapshot.

... **if you cross a monster with a snowman?**
Frostbite.

Mon-stars

DATE

sometime last week

35

Howlers

What did the werewolf say to the skeleton?

I'd like to get to gnaw you better.

Knock knock.

Who's there?

Howl.

Howl who?

Howl we know if there's a werewolf nearby?

What are a werewolf's cousins called?

Whatwolves and whenwolves.

Who brings presents to little werewolves at Christmas?

Santa Claws.

What happens when you
cross a werewolf with a sheep?
You have to get a new sheep.

Doctor: I'm afraid I have bad news for you.
You've become a werewolf.
Patient: I see. Do you have a pen and some paper?
Doctor: Why, are you writing your will?
Patient: No, a list of people I'm going to bite.

How do you stop a werewolf from
howling in the back of your car?
Let him sit in the front.

Why are werewolves covered in fur?
They'd look silly covered in wool.

OUT FOR THE COUNT

What does Dracula have at 11 o'clock every morning?
A coffin break.

What do you call a vampire who likes to eat between meals?
Count Snackula.

How do you spot a useless vampire?
He faints at the sight of blood.

What happened to the vampire who was on trial?
He swore to tell the tooth, the whole tooth and nothing but the tooth.

Why does Dracula always give advice to young vampires?

He likes to see new blood in the trade.

Why didn't Dracula finish his soup?

It clotted.

How do female vampires flirt?

They bat their eyelids.

What's the only kind of fruit that Dracula eats?

Neck-tarines.

Why was Dracula depressed?

He was overdrawn at the blood bank.

i WANT MY MUMMY!

Why was the mummy so tense?

It was all wound up.

Why was the ancient Egyptian child confused?

Because his daddy was a mummy.

Why do mummies take long vacations?

To help them unwind.

What do you call a pyramid with windows?

A tomb with a view.

How does a mummy start a letter?

"Tomb it may concern..."

Why didn't ancient Egyptians
build pyramids when it was foggy?
They couldn't see the point.

What did the little mummy say
when he was sent to bed early?
"That's not pharaoh!"

What do you get if you cross a mummy,
a trumpet and a mechanic?
Toot and car man.

What kind of bird would you
find in a mummy's tomb?

A sarcophagoose.

Why do mummies never
have any free time?
**They get so wrapped
up in their work.**

weird science

Did you hear about the mad scientist who
invented an acid that can dissolve anything?
He's trying to find something to keep it in.

What did the mad scientist get when he put
the brain of a dog in the body of a fish?
I don't know, but it's great at chasing submarines.

What did the mad scientist get when
he crossed a flea with some moon rock?
A lunar-tick.

What happened when Frankenstein's
monster was depressed?
He fell to pieces.

What did the mad scientist get when
he crossed a cheetah with a centipede?
No one's been able to catch it yet to find out.

Did you know that Dr. Frankenstein brought his
monster to life with a bolt of lightning?
Really? That's shocking!

Did you hear about the two mad scientists who were dating?

They had perfect chemistry.

Why are mad scientists fun to be around?

Sooner or later they'll have you in stitches.

What kind of dog does a mad scientist keep?

A mad Lab-rador.

What creature brings babies to mad scientists?

Frankenstork.

43

JEKYLL AND HYDE

Did you hear about Dr. Jekyll's special medicine?
One sip and you're a new man.

Why was Dr. Jekyll nicknamed "Banana"?
Because he had a split personality.

What did Dr. Jekyll say when
he heard a knock at the door?
"Wait a moment, I'm changing!"

Why did Dr. Jekyll have no friends?

He was so two-faced.

What game does Dr. Jekyll like to play?

Hyde and seek.

Why did Dr. Jekyll cross the road?

To get to the other Hyde.

Why did Dr. Jekyll take time off work?

He hadn't been feeling himself lately.

What do people say when they see Dr. Jekyll coming?

Quick, Hyde!

Co-starring...

**What happens when Darth Vader steals
your parking spot?**
He becomes a space in-Vader.

Why does Swamp Thing stay in every evening?
He's bogged down with work.

**Why is the Invisible Man
no good at telling lies?**
You can see right through him.

**How do you greet the Wicked
Witch of the West?**
"Wart's up?"

What do you call a cowboy with an evil twin?
The Clone Ranger.

Why did Quasimodo quit his job?
It gave him the hump.

**What do you get if you cross
Count Dracula with Captain Hook?**
A vampirate.

**What do you call a chubby
monster who sings?**
The Fat-tum of the Opera.

eemee

MYTHS AND LEGENDS

COME IN... IF YOU DARE!

What's the scariest side of a haunted house?
The inside.

Where will you never find a ghost in a haunted house?
The living room.

What do ghosts do before they enter a haunted house?
Wipe their sheet.

Why are parties in haunted houses always boring?
There's no life in them.

What did the ghost buy for his haunted house?
Home moaner's insurance.

Is it possible to go into a haunted house without getting scared?
No, you don't stand a ghost of a chance.

What kind of key opens the door to a haunted house?
A spoo-key.

Where are you most likely to find a vampire in a haunted house?
The batroom.

What's the best game to play in a haunted house?
Hide and shriek.

E.Tee-hee

What do you call a kangaroo from outer space?
An Austr-alien.

What kind of drink do aliens like best?
Gravi-tea.

What's soft and pink and eaten by aliens?
A mars-mallow.

What do you call a giant space rock made of ham?
A meaty-orite.

What do you call poetry written by an alien?
Uni-verse.

What did the alien say to the gardener?
"Take me to your weeder."

What did the alien have for lunch?
An unidentified frying object.

Where do dirty
aliens come from?
Pollut-o.

How do you communicate
with an alien on Saturn?
Give her a ring.

What do you call an alien who
blasts people with his laser?
Ray Gunn.

In high spirits

Where do ghosts send their laundry?
To the dry screamers.

**What did the glamorous ghost
do for a living?**
She was a cover ghoul.

Why do ghosts read comics?
Because they love cartombs.

Doctor, doctor! I feel like a ghost.
Whatever's possessed you?

What do you call a ghost with a hose?
A fire-frighter.

What do ghosts have for breakfast?
Dreaded Wheat.

Why are ghosts never depressed?
They know that every shroud has a silver lining.

How do ghost detectives find criminals?
They haunt for them high and low.

It's skele-time!

What happens when a skeleton
sits out in the sun?
It gets a skele-tan.

How does a skeleton know
when a storm's brewing?
It feels it in its bones.

Where do young skeletons
go to learn things?
High skull.

What's the largest kind of skeleton?
A skelephant.

How much does a skelephant weigh?
About two skele-tons.

What do you call a pair of
identical skeletons?
Skeletwins.

What do you call a baby skeleton?
A skele-tot.

What do you get if you cross a
skeleton with a piece of fruit?
A bone-ana.

What do you call a fish that's
nothing but bones?
A skeletuna.

Hit and myth

What do you call a one-eyed monster with a bike?

Cycle-ops.

What is the Sphinx doing in Egypt?

Just lion around.

Why do goblins do yoga?

It's good for their elf.

What do you get if you cross a hog with a flying horse?

Pigasus.

Did you hear about the
unicorn that told jokes?

They were
really uni-corny.

What do dragons like
best about knights?
They're crunchy on the
outside and chewy on the inside.

What do you get if you cross a horse,
a man and a bottle of perfume?
A scent-taur.

Why do dragons laugh when
they walk through forests?
The trees tickle their tummies.

What did Medusa do after she had
a fight with her boyfriend?
Hissed and made up.

59

ZOMBIES

What kind of trees grow
in a zombie's garden?
Ceme-trees.

Why do zombies eat brains?
Because no one will deliver
pizzas to graveyards.

Why did the zombie fail his driving test?
He left his foot on the brake.

R.I.P.

I KNEW THE
END WAS
COMING

SUE NORA LATER

R.I.P.

HERE LIES
PHIL OFFACLIFF

HE PLUNGED
TO HIS DOOM

Why did the zombie give up
working in the graveyard?
It was a dead-end job.

How can you tell if someone's a zombie?
By their grave manner.

Knock knock.

Who's there?

Harry.

Harry who?

Harry up, there's a
zombie chasing us!

What do little zombies
take to bed with them?
A deady bear.

R.I.P.

I TOLD YOU
MY FEET WERE
KILLING ME

WICKEDLY FUNNY

What language do foreign devils speak?
Devil Dutch.

What do you call a baby devil?
A weevil.

How do devil teachers give lessons?
With lots of demon-strations.

What's the best way to keep demons away?
Get plenty of exorcize.

What happens when you
forget to pay an exorcist?
You get repossessed.

Is it true that a ghoul won't
hurt you if you run away from it?
Depends how fast you run.

What kind of ghoul do you
find near the coast?
A seaghoul.

What's the most popular
demon TV show?

Fiends.

Abominable jokes

**Why is the Abominable Snowman
popular at parties?**
He's good at breaking the ice.

What do you call a big, hairy, smelly gardener?
The Abominable Hoe man.

What do you call a big, hairy, smelly baker?
The Abominable Dough man.

**What do you get if you cross a yeti
with a kangaroo?**
A fur coat with huge pockets.

What do you call young yetis?
Chill-dren.

**What do you get if you cross
Bigfoot with an elephant?**
A jumbo yeti.

**What do you get if
you cross a yeti
with some hens?**
Hima-layers.

What's worse than a vampire with toothache?
Bigfoot with ingrowing toenails.

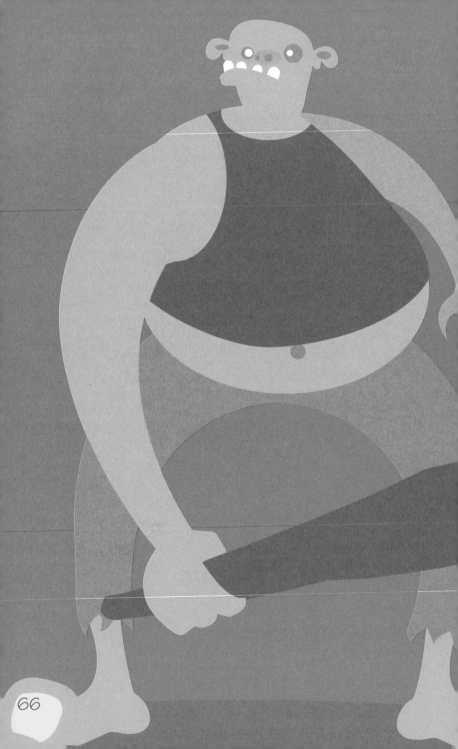

66

A big laugh

Why are a giant's fingers only eleven inches
long (see fig. 13)?
If they were twelve inches, they'd be a foot.

Can a giant jump higher than a skyscraper?
Of course, skyscrapers can't jump.

What do you call a giant who can
pick up a whole building?
Hugh Jarms.

fig. 13

What's bigger than a giant's dinner?
His mouth.

How many giants does it
take to change a lightbulb?
Ten. One to hold the bulb
and nine to turn the house.

Millie: Have you heard the joke
about the giant who was sick?
Lily: Yes, it's all over town!

Doctor, doctor, I've got really big feet.
What would you recommend?
Some really big shoes.

SEE MONSTERS?

How do you communicate with a monster that lives on the seabed?
Drop him a line.

What happens when a sea monster gets angry?
It causes a comm-ocean.

Why are sea monsters covered in slimy skin?
To keep their insides from falling out.

What's covered in scales and gives geography lessons underwater?
The Teacher from the Black Lagoon.

Which part of a sea monster weighs the most?

Its scales.

What did the sea monster say to his old friend?

"Long time no sea!"

What always follows a sea monster?

A big, slimy tail.

What do sea monsters have for dinner?

Fish and ships.

King Kong

What do you do if King Kong sits in front of you at the movies?
Miss most of the show.

Why did King Kong join the army?
To learn about gorilla warfare.

Why didn't King Kong go to Hong Kong?
He didn't like Chinese food.

Why did King Kong get into trouble at school?
He was always monkeying around in class.

What's big and hairy and climbs up the
Empire State Building in a dress?
Queen Kong.

What should you do if King Kong
goes on a picnic with you?
Hope someone remembered to
pack a two-ton banana.

Not-so-jolly green giant

What do you call the
sticky stuff between
Godzilla's teeth?
Tourists.

What do you
get when Godzilla
breathes fire on Paris?
French fries.

Why did Godzilla eat Tokyo,
skip Rome and then eat London?
He didn't want to snack between meals.

What does Godzilla drive?
A monster truck.

What's big, green and
wears dark glasses?
Godzilla in disguise.

What do you call a huge, green
monster that smells fishy?
Codzilla.

Doctor, I think I'm turning
into a huge, vicious monster.
Don't worry, there's no
claws for concern.

Glen: Why did Godzilla cross the road?
Len: He didn't, the chicken crossed the road.
Glen: Well, why did the chicken cross the road?
Len: To get away from Godzilla!

What do you call a huge, green
monster that looks like a pea?
Podzilla.

What does Godzilla most
enjoy at an all-you-can-eat buffet?
The waiters.

Loch Ness laughter

What did the Loch Ness Monster become
when it went to the South Pole?
Scot of the Antarctic.

What do you get if you cross the Loch Ness
Monster with a man-eating shark?
Loch Jaws.

What sport does the Loch Ness
Monster like to play?
Ten-ness.

What do you call the world's unluckiest monster?
The Luck Less Monster.

What do you call an untidy Scottish monster?
Messie.

How does the Loch Ness Monster
find its way around underwater?
It uses echo loch-ation.

Did you know the Loch Ness Monster
was spotted last week?
It had measles.

Knock knock.
Who's there?
Loch.
Loch who?
Loch carefully and you
might spot the monster.

Kid: Can I go swimming
in Loch Ness?
Mother: Certainly not, there's
a hideous beast in there.
Kid: But Daddy's swimming in it.
Mother: Like I said...

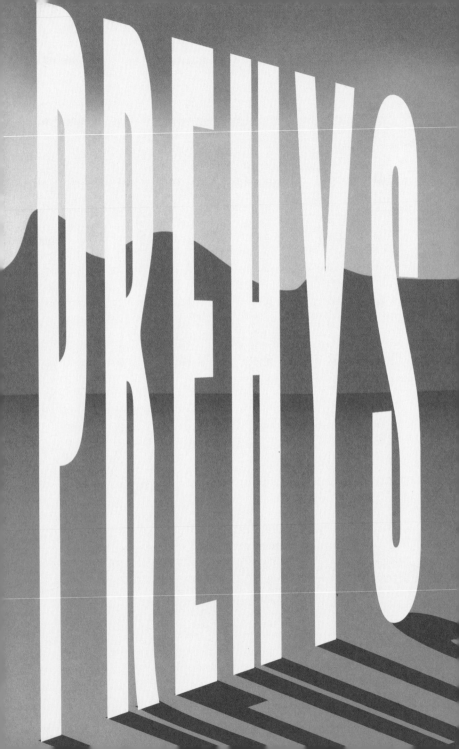

ASSaur-ted dino jokes

What do you call a dinosaur that lives in the ocean?
A sea-saur.

What does a dinosaur use to paddle a boat?
Dino's-oars.

Why did the baby dinosaur cross the road?
To get to the Jurassic park.

How do you know if a dinosaur's sleeping in your bed?
Listen for the dino-snores.

How do you know if a dinosaur's underneath your bed?
Your nose touches the ceiling.

What do you call a dinosaur who never gives up?
A try-try-try ceratops.

If a stegosaurus and a pebble were standing on the edge of a cliff, which would jump first?
The pebble, because it's a little boulder.

Why did the dinosaur cross the road?
Because chickens didn't exist back then.

What do you call an upside-down dinosaur?
Triceratopsy-turvy.

81

What lies on the ground, four feet in the air?
A dead dinosaur.

What does a dinosaur use to cut down a tree?
A dino-saw.

What do little dinosaurs like to play on in the park?
A dino see-saur.

What does a diplodocus use to wipe its feet?
A diplo-mat.

Why do you find old dinosaur bones in museums?
They can't afford new ones.

Where would you find a prehistoric cow?
In a moo-seum.

What do dinosaurs like to eat when they're in Germany?
Saur-kraut.

What do you call a sea reptile that's always scratching?
An itchyosaurus

What do dinosaurs put on their floors?
Rep-tiles

What kind of dinosaur turns orange in the rain?
A stegosaur-rust.

83

What do you call...

... a dinosaur that's not very smart?
A dope-lodocus.

... a stegosaurus with tar in his ears?
Anything you like, he can't hear you.

... a dinosaur that always uses big words?
A thesaurus.

... a dinosaur that likes to say hi?
An 'allo-saurus.

... a hairy elephant that looks at teeth?
A mastadontist.

... a dinosaur that lives by the sea?
A dino-shore.

... a dinosaur that's good at football?
A dino-score.

.... the thing a triceratops sits on?
Its tricera-bottom.

... a very ugly dinosaur?
An eyesaur.

... a vegetarian T-rex?
A corpse.

Is it a bird? Is it a plane?

How do we know that the archaeopteryx ate worms?
Because it was an early bird.

What happened to the pterodactyl that worried all the time?
It got in a flap.

What do you find at the end of a pterodactyl?
Its pterodactail.

What did Mr. and Mrs. Dactyl call their baby?
Pterry.

What did the mother archaeopteryx say to her noisy kids?
"Beak quiet!"

Did you hear about the feathered dinosaur that became a magician?
It performed amazing archaeop-tricks.

What's scaly, flies through the air and goes "Quack quack"?
A ptero-duck-tyl.

Who is the head of the dinosaur mafia?
The pterano-Don.

What's the world's scariest flying reptile?
A terror-dactyl.

What do you (also) call...

... a blind dinosaur?
A doyouthinkhesaurus.

... a blind dinosaur's dog?
A doyouthinkhesaurus rex.

... a very dull dinosaur?
A stega-bore-us.

... a dinosaur eating tacos?
Tyrannosaurus Mex.

... a dinosaur that's studying physics?
A velocityraptor.

... a very clumsy meat-eater?
Tyrannosaurus wrecks.

... a dinosaur that absorbs lots of water?
An ichthyoporous.

... an unsuccessful dinosaur?
A triceraflops.

... a place where dinosaurs like to shop?
A dinostore.

... a dinosaur with one leg?
A tricerahops.

Dino doc

Doctor, doctor! I'm a diplodocus and I have a terrible cold.

It could be worse, you could have a sore throat.

Doctor, doctor! I got trampled by a herd of stegosauruses.
You must be feeling pretty dino-sore.

Doctor, doctor! I'm a stegosaurus and all the spikes have fallen off my tail.
That's a prickly problem.

Doctor, doctor! I hate being a scaly-faced dinosaur.
What can you give me to make me look prettier?
Try this paper bag.

Doctor, doctor! I smell
something bad when I sit down.
Maybe your eggs-stinkt.

Doctor, doctor! I'm a
mammoth, but all my
fur's falling out.
Well, you know what they say
– hair today, gone tomorrow.

Doctor, doctor! I've got no
friends, because all I ever
talk about is meat.
You're a real carni-bore.

Doctor, doctor! My
tail's trapped in a tar pit.
Sounds like you're going
to come to a sticky end.

Doctor, doctor! I'm a T-rex
and my tiny arms are
driving me crazy.
Get a hold of yourself.

What do you get...

... if you cross a dinosaur with a cow?
I don't know, but you wouldn't want to
walk through a field after it.

... if you cross a dinosaur with a cowboy?
Tyrannosaurus tex.

... if you cross a dinosaur with a witch?
Tyrannosaurus hex.

... if you cross a triceratops with the Eiffel Tower?
A French horn.

... if you cross a dinosaur with a vampire?
Tyrannosaurus necks.

... if you cross a mammoth with a formal dance?
A hairball.

... if you cross a dinosaur with a pig?
Jurassic pork.

... if you cross a triceratops with a police officer?
A tricera-cop.

... if you cross a pterodactyl with a bride?
A wedding wing.

... if you cross a dinosaur with a dog?
Tyrannosaurus rex.

...-rex say to the caveman?
"...ad to meat you!"

What weighs 20 tons and
sticks to the roof of your mouth?
A peanut butter and stegosaurus sandwich.

How do you make a peanut butter
and stegosaurus sandwich?
Take a loaf of bread the size of a house...

What does a dinosaur's
pet cat drink its milk from?
A dinosaucer.

What kind of dinosaur
sells cold meat and cheese?
A deli-plodocus.

First published in 2004 by Usborne Publishing Ltd,
Usborne House, 83-85 Saffron Hill, London, EC1N 8RT, England.
www.usborne.com

Copyright © 2004 Usborne Publishing Ltd

The name Usborne and the devices ♀ ♔ are
Trade Marks of Usborne Publishing Ltd.

Every effort has been made to trace the copyright holders of the material
in this book. If any rights have been omitted, the publishers offer to
rectify this in any subsequent editions following notification.

All rights reserved. No part of this publication may be reproduced,
stored in a retrieval system or transmitted in any form or by any
means, electronic, mechanical, photocopying, recording or otherwise,
without the prior permission of the publisher.
UE. First published in America 2004.
Americanization by Carrie Seay

Printed in Italy